The Highlands of Scotland

A Jarrold Colour Publication

The Highlands of Scotland

with text by Lisa Newcombe

Arrochar on Loch Long.

THE SCOTTISH HIGHLANDS, a region unparalleled for stern grandeur, lie approximately to the north and west of a line joining the mouth of the Clyde with Stonehaven. There is, in fact, no fixed boundary, but the obvious definition of the Highlands as the mountainous area of Scotland is not strictly true, for the Lowlands also have many high mountains. Rather, the area could be defined as the last stronghold of the Gaelic tongue in Great Britain, although even this is now dying out.

The Highlands of Scotland contain some of the grandest scenery in the British Isles and the very mention of their name sends a succession of pleasing images flashing through the mind, invoking a picture of brooding, snow-capped mountains that rise steeply above a rushing torrent, or shy red deer cropping the sparse vegetation of the glens and hill-sides, ever alert to the dangers provoked by the intrusion of humans on their environment. The three most striking scenic features here are the mountains themselves, the lochs, and their river valleys. Though they would still be beautiful on their own, each is enhanced by the others. The mountain never achieves a nobler demeanour than when it rises above the calm waters of a loch, and the loch never touches us with a sharper sense of enchantment than when its serenity mirrors the image of some mighty ben.

The greatest mountain masses in the British Isles are situated in the Highlands, and more than 500 of them are over 3,000 feet high. (Ben Nevis, of course, is our highest peak at 4,406 feet.) There are two principal ranges, the Grampians and Druim Albain. Each mountain has a distinctive character of its own, formed after millions of years of erosion: some have menacing, jagged pinnacles that seem to be ever striving upwards; some are humpbacked and mis-shapen, or gently curved; while still others are capped with a snowy quartzite cone. The lochs, both freshwater and sea-inlets, are mostly long and narrow and they lie in deep basins gouged out by glacial action. The Highland rivers are quite different from the broad and rather sluggish rivers so often found in England. The largest Highland rivers are the Tay and the Dee, while the rest tend to be small but fast, bubbling and foaming as they rush through dramatic gorges on their way to a loch or the sea. Salmon can sometimes be glimpsed leaping rapids as they battle their way upstream. Pollution, fortunately, is almost unheard of here, and the only substance likely to tinge these crystal-clear waters is an occasional brown peat stain. The rapidity of some of these rivers is now finally being made use of in modern hydro-electric schemes.

Scotland's history stretches far back to the Stone Age, and scattered throughout the entire Highland region are the marks left by its sometimes peaceful, sometimes turbulent past. Scotland was first inhabited during the Neolithic Age and prehistoric traces such as chambered cairns can still be found. The Highlands were so remote then that they progressed at a slower rate than the rest of Great Britain, but their remoteness also had the advantage that the conquering Romans and later the Normans never infiltrated into the region. St Columba, who founded his church on Iona in 563, had a profound effect on Scotland's progress, for he spread Christianity, and with it the Gaelic language, through the Highlands.

While Scotland remained a separate kingdom, the Highland chieftains ruled their own lands with scant deference to the crown, and frequently quarrelled among themselves. But the English were the common enemy and the Highlanders bravely resisted the attempts of Edward I to subjugate them, and they succeeded in routing the English at Bannockburn in 1314. Robert the Bruce was responsible for this great victory, and so he ruled as undisputed king of Scotland till his death. In spite of union with the English crown in 1603 (when Mary

Queen of Scots' son ascended the English throne as James I), and with the English Parliament in 1707, the Highlanders continued to assert their independence. This led to the Jacobite rebellion of 1715 (inflamed by the Massacre of Glen Coe instigated by the English), which was put down at the battle of Sherrifmuir; and the more important Jacobite rising of 1745. Prince Charles Edward led his army of gallant Highlanders down into England, but they were forced to retreat and were finally defeated at Culloden. The romantic memory of Bonnie Prince Charlie still lives on, however, and a memorial has been erected at Glenfinnan, where he first unfurled his battle standard. The tragic 'Clearances' of the eighteenth and nineteenth centuries, when crofters were thrown out of their homes to make room for the more profitable herds of sheep, further weakened the influence of the Highland clans.

Despite the decline of the traditional clan (they were in danger of dying out completely until they began to come back into fashion after Queen Victoria displayed such enthusiasm for Scotland and all things Scottish), nowhere else in the British Isles are family ties more firmly established. The name 'clan', meaning 'children', was originally applied to a group claiming common ancestry who lived as a family on their own land under the leadership of their chief. Each clan, such as the powerful Campbells, Macdonalds and Camerons, have their own distinctive tartan, and although the members of clans are now often widely dispersed, they still proudly wear their tartan on festive occasions such as the traditional Highland Games, which are held at several centres each year.

Besides the incomparable scenery where history mingles with legend, the Highlands of Scotland have much to offer in the way of fauna. Sheep, of course, are numerous as are the splendid Highland cattle with their huge horns and long, reddish hair, but the visitors who are prepared to spend time and effort in exploring away from the main tourist routes may be rewarded with the sight of a herd of red deer, the occasional wild cat or marten, or even a majestic eagle swooping from the snowy heights of some mountain.

Among the main occupations in the Highlands today are farming or crofting, fishing at great and small ports alike, and some distillation of whisky. Hydro-electric schemes and extensive afforestation are helping to effect a recovery in the economic life here but the major industry is undoubtedly that of tourism, which has been thriving ever since Queen Victoria bought Balmoral and so popularised the region. Every effort is made to cater for the visitor, including the provision of facilities for sports ranging from mountaineering to water-skiing or fishing (many of the lochs and rivers are replete with salmon, sea-trout and brown trout.) One of the most popular tourist attractions are the Highland Games, which offer a unique chance to watch the 'tossing the caber' event or to listen to the emotive skirl of the pipes. Fortunately, despite this influx of tourists, the scenery here remains unspoilt and uncluttered, for there is space enough for everyone, and the future for the Highlands of Scotland, particularly since the recent development of the off-shore oil fields, looks bright indeed.

Strathclyde Region

The counties of Scotland have recently been rearranged and renamed. The new Strathclyde Region, which actually extends into the Lowlands, incorporates the former great county of Argyll and many of the Inner Hebridean Islands.

This was the original Scotland, for the Scots from Ireland settled here in the fifth century and named the kingdom Dalriada. The district was also the very cradle of Scottish Christianity and scattered throughout the county are the marks of over 2,000 years of Scottish history, including Celtic crosses, ruined old churches and even some prehistoric cairns.

The landscape of Strathclyde embodies every feature that one thinks of as typically Scottish. Here, there is rich and fertile land, ideal for cultivation; heather-clad hills and lonely moors; tumultuous streams foaming through narrow gorges; fabulous mountain peaks and an abundance of both freshwater lochs and sea-lochs. Indeed, the coastline of Strathclyde is deeply indented by its magnificent sea-lochs (including Loch Fyne, Loch Melfort and Loch Etive) which divide the district into great peninsulas such as Kintyre and Cowal. The attractive stretch of water known as the Firth of Clyde, a popular haunt of boating enthusiasts, separates the Cowal Peninsula from the lovely Isle of Arran.

Strathclyde's many islands complement its mainland scenery and are well worth a visit. They include the Isle of Arran, a beautiful holiday resort with marvellous scenic variety; the peaceful Islay and Jura; and Mull, one of the largest of the Inner Hebrides. This is a hilly island with an extremely irregular coastline indented by sea-lochs. The Sound of Iona separates Mull from the small island of Iona, known all over the world for its great cathedral, which dates mainly from the sixteenth century. St Columba came here from Ireland in 563 and founded a monastery – from this humble base he introduced the Christian religion to Scotland. The island possesses Scotland's earliest Christian burial ground, St Oran's Cemetery, and here are the tombs of many great chieftains and kings, including Duncan, who was reputedly murdered by Macbeth.

Loch Awe and Kilchurn Castle, with Ben Lui in the background.

Loch Awe et le château Kilchurn avec une vue du Ben Lui à l'arrière.

Loch Awe und Schloß Kilchurn; im Hintergrund Ben Lui.

I

Loch Eck is a charming loch encircled by tree-clad hills that rise abruptly from the water's edge (1). One of the highest peaks here is Bheinn Mhor (2,433 feet). This is a peaceful and secluded loch, with shores fringed with delicate fronds of the bracken that grows in such profusion throughout the Highlands. Eck is situated in the Cowal Peninsula, an area indented with great sea-lochs, which stretches from Loch Fyne to the Firth of Clyde. This has long been a favourite holiday centre for both the Scots and the Sassenachs, so the serenity of Loch Eck can easily be exchanged for the noise and bustle of Clydebank resorts such as Dunoon, the 'Capital of Cowal'.

Seen here from Arduaine on Loch Melfort, the island of Luing (2) is bathed in the golden glow of the setting sun. Scotland is renowned for its fantastic sunsets which transfigure the landscape and clothe it in an aura of mystery and romance. Luing, which lies just off the Strathclyde mainland, is about six miles long and its gentle slopes are pockmarked with slate quarries which provided much industry here in the past. A new breed of cattle, a combination of the long-haired and prodigiously horned Highland cattle with shorthorns, was also developed on the island in the 1950s. Luing can be reached by the Cuan ferry from the south end of Siel Island. Siel is separated from the mainland by the narrow Siel Sound, an arm of the Atlantic, and this is spanned by picturesque Clachan Bridge, designed by Telford in 1792. Clachan has thus achieved fame as being the only bridge to 'span the Atlantic'.

Loch Eck (1) est un loch séduisant, entouré de collines boisées qui se forment au bord de l'eau. Un des pics les plus hauts est le Beinn Mhor, 742 mètres. La route qui contourne le côté est du loch offre des vues splendides. Luing, que l'on voit ici au coucher du soleil (2), est une île de plus de neuf kilomètres et demi couverte de carrières d'ardoise. On développa ici l'élevage d'une nouvelle espèce de bétail il y a quelques années. Luing, que l'on peut accéder par ferry, se trouve à très peu de distance de l'intérieur et est séparé de l'île de Scarba par le Sound of Luing. Cette photographie a été prise d'Arduaine, sur le rivage de Loch Melfort.

Loch Eck (1) ist ein reizvoller See, von bewaldeten Hügeln umgeben, die von den Ufern ansteigen. Einer der höchsten Gipfel ist Beinn Mhor, 742 m. Die Straße um das östliche Ufer des Sees bietet unvergeßliche Aussichten. Luing, hier beim Sonnenuntergang gesehen (2), ist eine 10 km lange Insel, mit vielen Schieferbrüchen. Vor einigen Jahren wurde hier eine neue Rinderrasse gezüchtet. Luing, das man mit einer Fähre erreichen kann, liegt nicht weit vom Festland und ist von der Insel Scarba durch die Meerenge von Luing getrennt. Diese Aufnahme wurde von Arduaine am Ufer des Loch Melfort gemacht.

2

3

4

Goat Fell, 874 mètres, est le pic le plus haut de l'île d'Arran (3). Lamlash est le village le plus important d'Arran (4); ici l'on voit Holy Island de l'autre côté de la baie de Lamlash où la flotte Norse se rassembla après la bataille de Largs. Loch Etive est entouré de nombreuses montagnes impressionnantes telle Ben Cruachan (5), 1 124 mètres. Loch Tulla (6) se trouve au pied du Black Mount (le Mont noir) renommé pour ses forêts qui abritent des daims. Ce détroit, le Kyles of Bute (7), sépare l'île de Bute de la terre ferme. Oban est un centre touristique important avec un port pittoresque (8).

5

Goat Fell, 874 m, ist der höchste Gipfel der Insel Arran (3). Das wichtigste Dorf von Arran ist Lamlash; auf der anderen Seite der Bucht sieht man Holy Island (4), wo sich die norwegische Flotte nach der Schlacht bei Largs wieder sammelte. Loch Etive ist von imposanten Bergen, wie Ben Cruachan (5), 1 124 m, umgeben. Loch Tulla (6) liegt am Fuß des „Black Mount", der wegen seiner Wildforste bekannt ist. Die Kyles of Bute (7) ist eine Meerenge, die die Insel Bute vom Festland trennt. Oban ist ein großes Touristenzentrum; von seinem malerischen Hafen aus (8) kann man Dampferfahrten nach vielen abgelegenen Orten machen.

7

6

8

The island of Arran, which is about twenty miles in length, is separated from the Inner Hebrides by the Kintyre Peninsula. The scenery here is extraordinarily varied, combining aspects of both the Lowlands and the Highlands – Goat Fell (3), 2,866 feet, is its highest peak. Lamlash is the most populous village on Arran. Lamlash Bay was once used by the defeated Norse fleet as a rallying point after the battle of Largs, and here, also, Robert Bruce set sail on his expedition in 1307. Across the bay can be seen Holy Island (4).

Loch Etive (5) is a great sea inlet surrounded by rugged mountains, including Ben Cruachan (3,689 feet). The smaller Loch Tulla (6) sits at the foot of the Black Mount, famous for its deer forests. The island of Bute is separated from the mainland by the narrows of the Kyles of Bute (7), traversed by the Clyde steamers. The greatest touring and holiday centre in Strathclyde is Oban, often called the 'Charing Cross of the Highlands'. From Oban's busy and colourful harbour (8), steamer trips may be taken to the more remote isles such as Iona.

Pretty Glen Croe is dominated by the heights of Ben Arthur (2,891 feet), a favourite climbers' resort and a noted landmark (9). Ben Arthur is also known as the Cobbler, from the Gaelic *An Cobaileach*, which means the 'forked peak'. The two adjoining peaks are the Cobbler's daughter and his wife. At the town of Ardrishaig is the entrance to the Crinan Canal (10), which links Loch Fyne and the Firth of Clyde to the Sound of Jura and the Atlantic. The nine-mile-long canal, which was built by John Rennie in 1793, is still used by pleasure boats as it saves them the journey round the Mull of Kintyre. Inveroran, situated at the south end of Loch Tulla (11), was the birthplace of the great Highland poet Duncan Ban MacIntyre. Loch Creran (12) lies between Lochs Etive and Linnhe on the coast of Strathclyde, and acts as a boundary between the two mountainous areas of Appin and Benderloch. Barcaldine Castle stands by the shores of this loch.

9 11

10

Ben Arthur, 881 mètres, est souvent appelé le 'Savetier' (cobbler) et surplombe Glen Croe (9). A peu près quinze kilomètres d'eau constitue le canal de Crinan (10), qui fut commencé en 1793. Le canal est toujours utilisé et permet aux embarcations d'éviter le contour de Mull of Kintyre. Loch Tulla (11) se trouve sur la route en direction de Glen Coe. Tout près on trouve Inveroran, le lieu de naissance du poète des Highlands Duncan Ban McIntyre. Loch Creran (12) se trouve entre Loch Etive et Loch Linnhe et forme une borne entre les deux districts montagnards Appin et Benderloch. C'est sur le rivage de ce loch que se dresse le Château de Barcaldine.

Ben Arthur, 881 m, oft „Der Schuster" genannt, ist ein bekanntes Wahrzeichen; er überblickt das anziehende Glen Croe (9). Der 15 km lange Crinan Kanal (10) wurde 1793 begonnen, ist heute noch im Betrieb und erspart die Fahrt um das Mull of Kintyre. Loch Tulla (11) befindet sich an der Straße nach Glen Coe. In der Nähe liegt Inveroran, Geburtsort des Hochland-dichters Duncan Ban McIntyre. Loch Creran (12) liegt zwischen Loch Etive und Loch Linnhe und ist die Grenze der Berg-gebiete Appin und Benderloch. Schloß Barcaldine steht am Ufer dieses Sees.

12

Mull is the largest island of the Inner Hebrides, some thirty miles long, although it is so irregular in shape and indented by sea-lochs that its coastline measures almost 300 miles. The centre of the island is mountainous, its highest peak being Ben More (3,169 feet). Mull is separated from the mainland by the Firth of Lorne and the Sound of Mull, but it can be easily reached by steamer from Oban. This photograph (13) was taken at the hamlet of Lagganulva on the north-west coast of the island.

The magnificent sixteenth-century Dunderave Castle, once the stronghold of the MacNaughtons, stands on the shores of the great sea-inlet, Loch Fyne (14). This is the 'Doom Castle' of Neil Munro's novel. The wild and mountainous scenery of Glen Orchy extends from Dalmally to the Bridge of Orchy – here (15) the River Orchy tumbles over its rocky bed before it unites with the River Strae. Loch Eck (16) is situated in the Cowal Peninsula between Loch Fyne and the Clyde Estuary. It is dominated by Beinn Mhor (2,433 feet), but is also surrounded by gentler slopes clothed in the soft green of the Scottish spruce forests. Here (17) a sturdy little croft is sheltered by the heights of Beinn Na Cille, near Kingairloch.

14　15

Mull est l'île la plus grande des Hébrides de l'intérieur; elle est bien connue pour son paysage de montagnes et ses nombreux lochs paisibles. Cette photographie a été prise à Lagganulva (13). Le magnifique château du seizième siècle de Dunderave (14) se trouve sur les rivages de Loch Fyne. Ce château fut autrefois la forteresse de la famille MacNaughton. Cette photographie montre la rivière Orchy (15) qui coule sur un lit rocheux à travers le somptueux Glen Orchy . Loch Eck (16) à l'aspect désolé, sur la péninsule Cowal, est entouré de collines. Ici, (17) l'on voit un vigoureux petit cottage écossais, abrité par les hauteurs de Beinn Na Cille, près de Kingairloch.

17

Mull, die größte Insel der Inneren Hebriden, ist wegen ihrer bergigen Landschaft und der vielen friedlichen Seen berühmt. Diese Aufnahme wurde in Lagganulva gemacht (13). Das stattliche Schloß Dunderave (14) aus dem 16. Jahrhundert steht am Ufer des Loch Fyne, einer Meeresbucht. Dieses Schloß war einst die Festung der Familie Mac-naughton. Der einsame Loch Eck (16) auf der Halbinsel Cowal ist von düsteren Hügeln umgeben. Dieses Bild zeigt den Orchy (15), der auf seinem felsigen Flußbett durch das schöne Glen Orchy dahinfließt. Hier (17) sieht man ein stabiles, schottisches Bauernhäuschen, das von dem hohen Beinn Na Cille bei Kingairloch beschützt ist.

16

Balmaha lies on the shore of Loch Lomond, below Ben Lomond.
Balmaha s'étend sur la rive du Loch Lomond en dessous de Ben Lomond.
Balmaha liegt am Ufer des Loch Lomond unterhalb Ben Lomond.

Central Region

The new Central Region which extends into The Lowlands, now includes the former areas of Stirling, Clackmannan and Falkirk.

The Central Region is rich with historical associations, for this area played an important part in the early development of Scotland. The remains of the Antonine, or Roman, Wall, for instance, can still be seen here; as can Bannockburn, the site of the famous battle when the English were defeated by Bruce in 1314. At the great city of Stirling, 'Gateway to the Highlands', the fifteenth-century Old Bridge is still standing. This was once of great strategic importance, being the only exit to the north. The battle of Stirling Bridge, in which Wallace was victorious, was fought nearby.

However, the outstanding sights of the Central Region are really Loch Lomond and the gorge of the Trossachs. The Trossachs' unusual name means 'Bristly Country', a rather appropriate title for this lovely wooded defile that stretches between Loch Achray and Loch Katrine. The whole of the Trossachs district has strong connections with the great author Sir Walter Scott, who immortalised this area in many of his works. Loch Katrine, in particular, is identifiable as the setting for *The Lady of the Lake*; nor has Loch Lomond, the 'Queen of Scottish Lakes', been neglected by Scott. Loch Lomond obviously inspired Tobias Smollet too, for he enthusiastically praised its 'verdant islands that seem to float on its surface, affording the most enchanting objects of repose to the excursive view'.

This countryside, so beloved by the poets, was also the haunt of Rob Roy MacGregor, the near-legendary Scottish outlaw and yet another of Scott's subjects. Rob Roy (Gaelic for 'Red Robert') lived during the seventeenth century and carried out many a daring raid in his heyday, until he was finally pardoned in 1727. His memory still lingers on among these now peaceful lochs that were once the scenes of so much adventure.

Loch Lomond, the largest of all the Scottish freshwater lochs (18), is undoubtedly one of the most beautiful stretches of water in the Highlands. It is also the best known, due partly to its proximity to the great towns of Glasgow and the Clyde, and partly to the genius of Sir Walter Scott, who immortalised Loch Lomond in many of his works. This great loch, twenty-four miles long, has a scattering of tiny islands, on some of which are monastic remains, at its southern end. The northern scenery of the loch is wild and lonely while on the eastern shore the mountains reach down to the water's edge – towering above them all is Ben Lomond (3,192 feet), probably the most climbed of all the Highland mountains. Ben Lomond can also be viewed from the romantic and tree-fringed Loch Ard, near the holiday centre of Aberfoyle, seen here with the sunlight glimmering on its calm waters (19). The road around the loch runs through the Pass of Aberfoyle.

West of Aberfoyle, the Menteith Hills look down on the Lake of Menteith, the only natural Scottish lake which is not known as a loch. On one of its three little islands, the Isle of Rest, stand the ruins of the early thirteenth-century Inchmahome Priory, where the five-year-old Mary Queen of Scots was placed in safe-keeping after the Battle of Pinkie in 1547. Inch Talla, a smaller island, holds the ruins of the ancient castle of the Earls of Menteith, while the third island, Dog Island, was used for kennels. Port of Menteith (20) is a little holiday resort and fishing centre (some fine pike can be caught here) which lies on the north-eastern shore of the lake. Beside its church is the mausoleum of the Grahams of Gartmore. The Menteith Hills are within the Queen Elizabeth Forest Park, which extends from the upper reaches of the River Forth to Loch Lomond.

18

Loch Lomond est très certainement un des plus beaux lacs de Grande-Bretagne et c'est aussi son plus long cours d'eau naturelle, trente-neuf kilomètres. Ben Lomond couronne le loch au-dessus avec ses 973 mètres (18). Loch Ard (19), que l'on voit ici avec les lueurs de soleil scintillant sur ses eaux calmes est un loch plein de charme entouré de collines boisées. Le port de Menteith (20) se trouve sur le rivage nord du lac de Menteith. C'est sur une île de ce lac qu'il y a les ruines du prieuré Inchmahome du treizième siècle.

Loch Lomond, ohne·Zweifel einer der schönsten Seen Großbritanniens, ist auch unser größter Frischwassersee mit einer Länge von 39 km. Hoch über dem See ragt Ben Lomond, 973 m (18). Hier sieht man Loch Ard (19), auf dem ruhigen Wasser schimmern die Sonnenstrahlen; es ist ein reizender, von bewaldeten Hängen umgebener See. Der „Port of Menteith" (20) steht auf dem nördlichen Ufer des „Lake of Menteith". Auf einer Insel im See stehen die Ruinen des Klosters Inchmahome aus dem 13. Jahrhundert.

20

21

22

Le petit Loch Doine (21) est séparé de son voisin Loch Voil par une
étroite bande de terre. Un beau, mais austère paysage entoure Loch
Iubhair (22). Tout près est le charmant village de Crianlarich. Loch
Chon, dont les rives sont bien boisées (23), s'étend entre les Lochs Ard
et Katrine au cœur de pays de Rob Roy. Ce hors-la-loi bien connu est
enterré à Balquhidder, à l'est de Loch Voil (24). Loch Katrine (25) est
le décor du roman de Sir Walter Scott *La Dame du Lac*. C'est main-
tenant un réservoir d'eau pour Glasgow. Loch Lubnaig, le « loch
arqué », peut être atteint par la passe rocheuse de Leny (26).

23

Der kleine Loch Doine (21) ist von seinem größeren Nachbarn, Loch
Voil, durch eine Landenge getrennt. Eine schöne, schroffe Landschaft
umgibt Loch Iubhair (22). In der Nähe steht das hübsche Dorf Crianlarich. Loch Chon, mit seinen dicht bewaldeten Ufern (23), liegt
zwischen Loch Ard und Loch Katrine im Herzen des „Rob Roy"-
Gebiets. Der bekannte Geächtete Rob Roy ist in Balquhidder, östlich
des Loch Voil (24), beigesetzt. Loch Katrine (25) war der Schauplatz
von Sir Walter Scotts *The Lady of the Lake*. Jetzt ist es ein Reservoir
für die Wasserversorgung Glasgows. Loch Lubnaig, „den krummen
See", kann man durch den felsigen Pass von Leny erreichen (26).

25

24

This is a district scattered with numerous enchanting lochs: Loch Doine, for instance (21), a small loch which is separated from Loch Voil by a neck of land. The road leads to Inverlochlaraig, where Rob Roy's house is situated, and where he died in 1734. Rob Roy (Robert MacGregor) was actually buried in the churchyard at Balquhidder, on the east shore of Loch Voil (24), so naturally this delightful loch has many associations with the famous outlaw. Here, the steep ridge known as the Braes of Balquhidder sweeps down to the tree-fringed shores.

Loch Iubhair (22), near Crianlarich village, is surrounded by fine, rugged scenery and bordered by Glen Dochart. Its unusual name means the 'Juniper' loch. Wild Loch Chon lies between Lochs Ard and Katrine, in the heart of Rob Roy country (23). These waters are a paradise for fishermen.

Loch Katrine (25), although very lovely in its own right, owes much of its fame to Sir Walter Scott, who used it as the romantic setting for his great work *The Lady of the Lake*. The level of the loch was recently raised, submerging the 'silver strand' described by Scott, and it is now a reservoir supplying Glasgow with water. Scott is still commemorated here, however, by the steamer bearing his name which plies the loch. Nearby is Glengyle, birthplace of Rob Roy, which can be visited by those travelling on the steamer. The gaunt Ben Venue (2,393 feet) towers overhead and Loch Katrine is bordered by the magnificently wooded and mountainous Trossachs ('bristly country') region, of which it was once remarked: 'The Trossachs beggar all description.'

From the popular resort of Callander (famous as the television film location for *Dr Finlay's Casebook*), the visitor should travel through the beautiful rocky gorge known as the Pass of Leny, where the Falls of Leny are situated. At the end of this pass, the River Leny reaches Loch Lubnaig (26), the 'bent loch'. Lubnaig is a long, narrow and wonderfully peaceful stretch of water which is noted for its fishing.

Ben Venue casts its brooding reflection in the waters of little Loch Achray (27). The gorge of the Trossachs extends from Loch Achray to Loch Katrine. Nearby is the 'Pass of the Cattle' used formerly by the MacGregors when they returned from plundering cattle in the Lowlands. The popular touring centre of Callander (28) is often referred to as the 'Gateway to the Trossachs', and the River Teith flows through this attractive town, having begun its journey at Loch Vennachar, to the west. Vennachar (29), described in Sir Walter Scott's *Lady of the Lake*, is one of the most delightful lochs in the Trossachs region.

Glen Dochart (30) was chosen by the poet James Hogg ('the Ettrick Shepherd') as the setting for his 'Spectre of the Glen'. Here, the River Dochart twists its way towards Loch Tay. The picturesque Falls of Dochart (31) are situated near Killin village, and by the Dochart Bridge (built in 1760) is the ancient burial place of Clan MacNab on the tiny island of Inch Buie. The River Dochart rises near the mountaineering and winter sports resort of Tyndrum (32), which is surrounded in every direction by fine mountains such as Ben Lui, Ben More, Beinn Oss and Beinn Odhar. The snow-covered slopes of the latter, 2,948 feet high, are shown in this photograph.

27

28

30

Le magnifique petit Loch Achray est surplombé du Ben Venue (27). Callander, portail des Highlands, est un centre de tourisme populaire (28). Loch Vennachar (29) est un des principaux attraits de la région des Trossachs. La rivière Dochart serpente à travers le pittoresque Glen Dochart (30) en direction du Loch Tay tandis qu'à Killin se trouvent les chutes de Dochart (31) et le pont Dochart, construit en 1760. Beinn Odhar se tourne vers le bas sur le hameau de Tyndrum (32), qui s'incruste commodément dans un espace de collines, toutes de plus de 760 mètres.

Der kleine, schöne Loch Achray wird von Ben Venue (27) überblickt. Callander, das Tor zu den Trossachs und dem Hochland, ist ein beliebter Touristenort (28). Loch Vennachar (29) ist eine der Hauptattraktionen des Trossach-Gebiets. Die Dochart schlängelt sich durch das malerische Glen Dochart (30) nach Loch Tay. In Killin sind die Dochart-Wasserfälle (31) und die 1760 erbaute Dochart-Brücke. Beinn Odhar blickt auf das schläfrige Dörflein Tyndrum (32); Tyndrum hockt mitten in den Bergen, die alle über 760 m hoch sind.

31

32

29

Tayside Region

The new Tayside Region includes Angus, Perth, Kinross and the great city of Dundee, which actually lies in The Lowlands.

Tayside is an area of unrivalled magnificence, where desolate peat moors give way to lush pastures and sombre forests while mountain peaks tower broodingly above clear, reed-fringed lochs. Indeed, Tayside's delightful lochs and river valleys are its most memorable feature, for the district encompasses Loch Rannoch, Loch Tummel, Loch Earn, the new Loch Faskally and, of course, Loch Tay itself. The great River Tay, the largest in Scotland, flows from the loch down to the 'Fair City' of Perth. This is a truly historic city, which became a royal burgh in 1210 and was for more than a century the capital of Scotland, until the court moved to Edinburgh after the assassination of James I in 1437.

Tayside has many other reminders of distant centuries besides Perth. Here are the remains of ancient fortresses and churches while many noble castles, such as Glamis, still stand. Here also is the Pass of Killiecrankie, once the scene of a formidable battle. The past, however, has not been allowed to usurp the present – modern development in the form of the Tummel/Garry hydro-electric scheme has been introduced into the district but has fortunately not been allowed to detract from its charm.

Apart from its scenic splendour, Tayside has much to offer the visitor. There are, for instance, many beautiful gardens and mansions open to the public, while the theatre-lover can attend a variety of performances at the much-acclaimed 'Theatre in the Hills' at Pitlochry. The more energetic visitor has not been forgotten – Tayside is particularly renowned for its angling waters but there are few sports which are not available. Facilities are provided for curling, skiing, pony-trekking and golf, while hill-walkers have unlimited scope among the gentler slopes and the more advanced climbers can tackle the heights of Ben Lawers.

The Blairgowrie to Braemar Road, Glen Shee.
La route de Blairgowrie à Braemar, Glen Shee.
Die Straße von Blairgowrie nach Braemar im Glensheetal.

33

Cette route (33) qui relie Blairgowrie à Braemar est la route principale la plus haute de Grande-Bretagne. Elle grimpe Glen Shee (34) et passe le Spittal de Glen Shee qui se trouve en tête de trois glens. La magnifique Passe de Killiecrankie (35) fut la scène d'une grande bataille en 1689, lorsque les troupes du Roi William furent mises en déroute par les jacobites.

Diese Straße (33), die Blairgowrie mit Braemar verbindet, ist die höchste Landstraße Großbritanniens. Sie steigt nach Glen Shee (34) und geht am „Spittal of Glen Shee", wo sich drei Täler treffen, vorbei. Hier stand einst ein Hospiz für Reisende. Der wunderschöne Killiecrankie-Pass (35) war 1689 Schauplatz einer großen Schlacht, als König Williams Truppen von den Jakobiten in die Flucht geschlagen wurden.

35

34

The mountain road linking Blairgowrie to Braemar on Royal Deeside is the highest main road in Great Britain, reaching a maximum height of 2,199 feet at the Cairnwell Pass, and encompassing wild and awe-inspiring moorland scenery (33). This road ascends Glen Shee (34) and passes the Spittal of Glen Shee at the head of three glens, where a hospice for travellers was originally situated – it is now an hotel. On the banks of the River Shee is an ancient stone circle and a tumulus known as Diarmid's Tomb.

One of Scotland's most attractive passes is the Pass of Killiecrankie (35), which is now the property of the National Trust. Few scenes today could present a more peaceful aspect as the River Garry flows gently through the fine wooded gorge, yet Killiecrankie was the site of a dramatic battle in 1689, when King William's troops were routed by the Jacobites, led by 'Bonnie Dundee' (Graham of Claverhouse) who was himself slain in the foray. One of the king's men escaped by leaping across the gorge at a point known ever since as 'Soldier's Leap'.

36

37

38

Milton of Clova (36) est un hameau désolé dans les montagnes sauvages du Glen Clova. On y trouve les ruines du château qui abrita Charles II en 1650. Les eaux du Loch Rannoch (37) sont utilisées comme réservoir et on trouve ici une station génératrice. Tout près s'étend le pauvre Moor of Rannoch parsemé de marécages tandis que sur ses rivages sud s'étend le Black Wood of Rannoch, un espace couvert en abondance de pins écossais. Loch Tummel (38) fait partie du plan hydro-électrique Tummel/Garry, mais toutefois il a conservé toute sa beauté. Loch Tummel est situé an centre d'un paysage de montagnes, dont le pic le plus impressionnant est le Schiehallion qui a 1 081 mètres et qui est surmonté d'un cône de quartz enneigé. C'est de Queen's View (39) sur les rives de Loch Tummel, endroit visité par la reine Victoria en 1866, que l'on voit le mieux Schiehallion.

Milton of Clova (36), ein einsames Dörfchen mitten im wilden felsigen Glen Clova. Hier stehen die Ruinen eines Schlosses, wo Charles II 1650 wohnte. Die Gewässer des 16 km langen Loch Rannoch (37) dienen als Reservoir für ein großes Kraftwerk. In der Nähe liegt das öde Moor of Rannoch, mit verstreut gelegenen Torfmooren; der „Black Wood of Rannoch", ein dichter Kiefernwald, begrenzt das Südufer des Sees. Loch Tummel (38) und Loch Rannoch bilden einen Teil des Wasserkraftsystems Tummel-Garry, glücklicherweise ist seine Schönheit unverdorben. Loch Tummel liegt mitten in einer hohen Berglandschaft; der auffallendste Gipfel ist Schiehallion, 1 081 m, der von einem schneeweißen Quarzitkegel gekrönt ist. Die beste Aussicht auf Schiehallion hat man von „Queen's View" (39) am Ufer des Loch Tummel, den die Königin Victoria 1866 besuchte.

The long valley of Glen Clova is encircled at its head by the Braes of Angus mountains, leading into the heart of the Grampians. The twin-peaked Lochnager lies to the north and the South Esk River meanders through the glen. Milton of Clova (36) is a tiny village here – nearby are the remains of an ancient castle where Charles II once stayed.

The waters of Loch Rannoch (37) ten miles in length, have now been utilised as a power reservoir and a large power station has been built at the western end of the loch. Despite this introduction of industry to the district, Loch Rannoch is blessed with a variety of delightful scenery. To the south are the peaks of Carn Mairg, Gairbh Mheall and Schiehallion, while the shores here are bordered by the Black Wood of Rannoch, dense with Scots pines. These ancient trees are a relic of the Caledonian Forest. The Moor of Rannoch to the west, also originally a pine forest, is now a vast and desolate expanse of peat bogs, rocks and the occasional stretch of water, such as Loch Laidon and Loch Ba. A railway, which was erected with the greatest difficulty on this soft ground and is forced to run on a causeway in places, traverses the moor.

Loch Tummel, shown here as the sun sinks behind its brooding mountains (38), forms part of the Tummel/Garry hydro-electric scheme. This necessitated the lengthening of the loch but, fortunately, its beauty is unspoilt. The best viewpoint of the loch can be obtained from Queen's View (39) to the east, which was visited by Queen Victoria in 1866. From here, one can gaze across the water towards Schiehallion (3,547 feet), surmounted by a snowy quartzite cone. This mountain was used by Maskelyne in an experiment in 1774 relating to the gravity of the earth.

39

Loch Tay, renowned for its fine salmon and trout fishing, is some fifteen miles in length with a depth of over 500 feet in places. Indeed, it is reputed to hold a larger volume of water than any other Scottish loch. To its north is the impressive mass of Ben Lawers (40) which, at 3,984 feet, is the highest mountain in the district. Despite its great height, however, Ben Lawers (its name means the 'echoing mountain') can be quite easily ascended and, when the weather conditions are favourable, skiers can sometimes be seen on its slopes. The panoramic views from the summit include a part of the Grampian range. Good roads run along both the shores of Loch Tay: that on its attractively wooded southern shore in particular offers a superb view over the serene water (41). The great River Tay flows from the east end of the loch to begin its 120-mile-long journey through Scotland.

Loch Tay, avec ses vingt-quatre kilomètres de long et une profondeur de 175 mètres, est reconnu avoir le plus important volume d'eau de tous les lochs écossais. Il est également renommé pour la pêche et surtout pour le saumon (40). Le haut pic de Ben Lawers, 1 214 mètres, domine son rivage nord tandis que le côté sud est plus paisible. Des routes parcourent les rivages nord et sud (41).

Der 24 km lange und über 175 m tiefe Loch Tay soll die größte Wassermenge aller schottischen Lochs enthalten. Er ist bekannt wegen seiner guten Angelgewässer (40), besonders für den Lachsfang. Der große Gipfel des Ben Lawers, 1 214 m, beherrscht sein Nordufer, während an der Südseite die Landschaft etwas sanfter ist (41). Straßen laufen an beiden Ufern entlang.

41

42

43

Peu de vallées d'Ecosse sont aussi belles que celle de la Tummel près de Pitlochry (42). A la suite de la construction d'un barrage à Pitlochry un nouveau loch, Faskally, a été créé, qui a été muni d'échelles de saumon (43). Un des affluents de la Tummel est la rivière Garry que l'on voit ici à Pitagowan (44). Un des châteaux les plus importants d'Ecosse est celui de Glamis (45), où est née la Princesse Margaret en 1930. Loch Earn (46) est un endroit populaire pour l'escalade et le sport. St Fillans (47) se trouve à l'extrémité est du loch, près du château d'Edinample qui date du dix-septième siècle.

Wenige Flußtäler in Schottland sind schöner als das des Tummel (42) bei Pitlochry. Durch den Bau einer Talsperre in Pitlochry ist der neue Loch Faskally entstanden, der mit Lachsleitern ausgestattet ist (43). Ein Nebenfluß der Tummel ist die Garry (44), hier bei Pitagowan aufgenommen. Eines der prächtigsten schottischen Schlösser ist Glamis (45), der Sitz der Grafen von Strathmore. Hier wurde die Prinzessin Margaret 1930 geboren. Der 10 km lange Loch Earn (46) ist eine beliebte Erholungsstätte für Angler und Bergsteiger. St. Fillans (47) liegt am östlichen Ende des Sees nahe Schloß Edinample, das aus dem 17. Jahrhundert stammt.

44

46

45

Few river valleys in the Highlands are more beautiful than that of the Tummel (42), near Pitlochry. This attractive holiday resort, said to mark the exact centre of Scotland, is the home of the 'Theatre in the Hills', Pitlochry's Festival Theatre, which presents a wide variety of concerts and plays during the summer months. There have been extensive hydro-electric developments in this area in recent years and a new loch, Faskally, has been created as a result of the construction of the Pitlochry Dam. Salmon ladders and an observation chamber have been provided at the dam (43) so that visitors can watch the amazing leaps of the adult salmon as they struggle towards their spawning grounds in the upper reaches of the river. One of the tributaries of the Tummel is the picturesque River Garry, seen here at Pitagowan (44), five miles east of the village of Blair Atholl. Ben Vrackie (2,333 feet), overlooks Glen Garry.

Loch Earn (46), six miles in length, is a popular sporting resort, which includes angling, boating, water-skiing and, of course, climbing among its attractions. The Scottish Championships are held here. At its western extremity is the village of Lochearnhead and here is the site of the now-ruined St Blane's Chapel. St Fillans (47), at the east end of the loch, also has a ruined chapel; the burial place of the Stewarts of Ardvorlich. St Fillans is another favourite haunt of sailing enthusiasts.

Probably the most famous castle in Scotland is that of Glamis (45), the seat of the Earl of Strathmore and the birthplace of Princess Margaret in 1930. Macbeth was supposedly Thane of Glamis, and this seventeenth-century, baronial-style castle certainly has many romantic and historic associations. The Elder Pretender, for example, held court here in 1715. Glamis is apparently haunted and legend has it that a sealed room in one of the towers imprisons a hideous monster.

Le village de Blair Atholl se trouve au croisement de la rivière Tilt avec la Garry, et possède le Glen Tilt à son nord. On peut voir ces chutes près du vieux pont de Tilt (48). Le château Blair vaut aussi la peine d'être visité. Il a été le siège des ducs d'Atholl depuis le treizième siècle. Le château Huntingtower (49) a été à une certaine époque la demeure de la famille Ruthven et il fut le décor du raide de Ruthven en 1582 lorsque le roi James VI y fut gardé prisonnier. La légende raconte que la première fille du comte a sauté d'une tour à l'autre pour rencontrer son amant.

Das Dorf Blair Atholl steht am Zusammenfluß der Tilt und der Garry, mit Glen Tilt im Norden. Diesen tosenden Wasserfall (48) sieht man bei der alten Brücke von Tilt. Schloß Blair ist auch sehenswert; seit dem 13. Jahrhundert ist es der Sitz der Herzöge von Atholl. Schloß Huntingtower (49) war einst der Wohnsitz der Familie Ruthven; im Jahre 1582 war es der Schauplatz des Überfalls von Ruthven, als König James VI hier in Gefangenschaft war. Das Gebäude ist zum Teil aus dem 17. Jahrhundert mit zwei Türmen aus dem 15. Jahrhundert. Der Sage nach soll die Tochter des ersten Grafen von einem Turm zum anderen gesprungen sein, um ihren Buhlen zu treffen.

48

The pleasant village of Blair Atholl is situated at the conjunction of the River Tilt with the Garry. Glen Tilt is a magnificent rocky glen stretching for almost six miles into the mountains of the Forest of Atholl, where the most impressive sight is the three-peaked Ben-y-Gloe, 'Mountain of the Mist', whose highest point is 3,671 feet. At the mouth of the glen, near the old Bridge of Tilt, are the Falls of Fender, where the icy-cold waters cascade over mossy stones, fringed by the myriad tints of the overhanging trees which cling defiantly to the steep and slippery bank (48).

Huntingtower Castle (49), three miles to the north of Perth, has an immensely colourful and dramatic history. Once the home of the Ruthven family (later Earls of Gowrie), it was the scene of the audacious 'Raid of Ruthven' in 1582. The young James VI was invited to Ruthven by the Earl of Gowrie who, with the help of other nobles, then held James prisoner for a time in an attempt to break the influence over him of the Royal favourites, the Earl of Arran and the Duke of Lennox. The Earl of Gowrie was later beheaded for his part in the 'Raid' and the building was renamed Huntingtower. It consists of two fifteenth-century tower houses, now restored, which are joined by a seventeenth-century portion. Legend relates that the daughter of the first Earl actually leapt between these two towers to avoid being caught with her lover, of whom her father disapproved. Tragically, she later threw herself off the tower and was killed, but the space between the towers is still known as the 'Maiden's Leap'. The house is now open to the public and contains much of interest, including early wall and ceiling paintings in the main hall.

Glen Muick, near Balmoral.
Glen Muick, près de Balmoral.
Glen Muick bei Balmoral.

Grampian Region

The Grampian Region now incorporates the districts of Moray, Banff, and parts of Aberdeen, Kincardine and Deeside.

This is a mainly agricultural and pastoral area, with many fishing villages scattered around its coastline, as well as the important herring fishing ports of Peterhead and Fraserburgh. Its most distinctive feature is, of course, the magnificent Grampian range from which it takes its name. This vast complex of mountains, covered in grass and heather, stretches across Scotland from the Strathclyde Region to the Grampian Region, and it also includes the ranges of the Cairngorms and the Monadhliaths.

Down the massive heights of the Grampians tumble many a Highland stream, including the Rivers Dee and Don. The Dee is really the life-blood of the district for it soon widens out into a broad and beautiful stretch of water, replete with salmon, which eventually flows into the sea at Aberdeen. The wooded valley of the Dee has earned the title 'Royal Deeside' for here is situated the Royal castle of Balmoral, the most famous of the region's many baronial castles. Balmoral was acquired and rebuilt by Queen Victoria, who fell under the spell of the rugged surrounding scenery. Indeed, it was her patronage that first brought fame and popularity to Deeside. She inadvertently started a fashion, known as 'Balmoralism', for all things Scottish, and so laid the foundations for the present flourishing tourist industry in the Highlands. The Royal Family still visit Balmoral every year, and worship at nearby Crathie church.

Aberdeen, the 'Granite City', is the capital of the Grampian Region and lies on the estuaries of the Rivers Dee and Don. In this ancient royal burgh, the old blends harmoniously with the new; and it can boast a cathedral and a university as well as being an important fishing port, an exporter of granite and cattle and a popular holiday resort.

The Royal Deeside resort of Braemar really consists of two separate parts, one on each side of the Clunie Water. On the west bank is Auchindryne, originally the Catholic sector, and on the east bank is Castleton, originally Protestant. The Braemar Gathering, an important event usually attended by the Royal Family, is held here in the Princess Royal Park every September and includes traditional Highland games in its programme. In Braemar itself are the ruins of a fourteenth-century hunting lodge, Kindrochit Castle, while just outside the village, near the conjunction of the Dee with the Clunie, stands Braemar Castle (50). The castle was built in 1628 by the Earl of Mar, burnt in 1689 and rebuilt in 1748 as an English garrison post by the Hanoverians. It is an excellent example of a Scottish fortified dwelling and this closer view (51) shows its eight-pointed enclosing wall, defiant towers and corbelled turrets. Sometimes open to the public, it is now the home of the Farquharson family and contains many interesting paintings.

The village of Crathie, Royal Deeside, is situated to the east of Balmoral Castle and encircled by heather-clad hills. The main feature of Crathie is its kirk (52), built in 1895, which is attended by the Royal Family when they are in residence at Balmoral. Queen Victoria, who also worshipped here, laid its

50

51

foundation stone. Near the river are the ruins of an earlier church, and here in the churchyard is a monument erected by Queen Victoria in memory of her ghillie, John Brown, who died in 1883.

Le château Braemar, qui se dresse près de la rivière Clunie tout près de son point de rencontre avec la Dee, fut construit par le Comte de Mar en 1628; c'est un exemple typique des demeures fortifiées écossaises (50). Cette vue plus proche du château (51) montre mieux le mur le contournant. Il date du milieu du dix-huitième siècle et est de nos jours la demeure de la famille Farquharson. Crathie est un village près du château de Balmoral qui est surtout connu pour son église de la fin du dix-neuvième siècle (52), laquelle est fréquentée par la famille royale lorsque celle-ci est en résidence à Balmoral.

Schloß Braemar liegt an dem Zusammenfluß der Clunie mit der Dee und wurde 1628 von dem Grafen von Mar gegründet. Es ist ein gutes Beispiel einer schottischen Festung (50). Ein näherer Blick (51) zeigt eine umschließende Mauer mit ihren drohenden Türmen. Das heutige Gebäude stammt aus der Mitte des 18. Jahrhunderts und ist jetzt der Wohnsitz der Familie Farquharson. Crathie, ein kleines Dorf in der Nähe von Balmoral, in der „Royal Deeside", ist wegen seiner Kirche (52) aus dem späten 19. Jahrhundert bekannt. Wenn die königliche Familie am Orte ist, besucht sie oft den Gottesdienst in dieser Kirche.

52

53

54

Glen Clunie (53), parsemé de minuscules fermes, est un endroit esseulé et paisible. Le Clunie Water (54) rejoint finalement la rivière Dee à Braemar. Cette photographie (55) montre la confluence de la Dee avec un autre de ses affluents, la Quoich, juste au-dessus de Braemar au bord de la forêt Mar. Près d'Invercauld le vieux pont de Dee traverse la rivière (56). Ce pont fut construit par le Général Wade au dix-huitième siècle dans l'intention de donner un accès militaire aux Highlands. Il a résisté aux puissantes inondations hivernales depuis plus de 200 ans. Invercauld House (57) jouit d'une position magnifique au nord de la rivière.

55

Das mit kleinen Bauernhöfen besäte Glen Clunie (53) ist eine einsame und friedliche Gegend. Das „Clunie Water" (54) fließt bei Braemar in den großen Dee-Fluß. Diese Aufnahme (55) zeigt den Zusammenfluß der Dee mit einem anderen Nebenfluß, dem Quoich, oberhalb Braemar am Rande des Marwaldes. Nebenan in Invercauld wird der Fluß von der Old Bridge of Dee (56) überspannt. Diese Brücke wurde im 18. Jahrhundert von General Wade erbaut, um Zugang für das Militär in das Hochland zu ermöglichen. Seit über 200 Jahren überstand diese Brücke die mächtigen Winterfluten. Invercauld House (57) ist nördlich des Flusses schön gelegen.

56

Glen Clunie (53), dotted with tiny farm buildings, is a quiet and peaceful spot which contrasts effectively with the foaming and tumbling Clunie Water (54) rushing through the glen. The Clunie Water eventually joins the Dee at Braemar, a village renowned for its invigorating air. Here, Robert Louis Stevenson wrote part of *Treasure Island*. The River Dee flows through the long and wooded valley known as Royal Deeside, and here we see the confluence of the Dee and its tributary the Quoich (55) just above Braemar, on the edge of Mar Forest.

Some six miles beyond Balmoral is Invercauld, where the Old Bridge of Dee spans the river (56). This bridge was built by General Wade in the eighteenth century and was designed to give military access to the Highlands. The bridge has stood firmly for over 200 years, for its immensely strong buttresses have been able to withstand the Dee's powerful winter floods. It is now royal property and a new bridge has been built a short distance to the west. Invercauld House, pictured here framed by trees (57), lies to the north of the river. The main part of this ancient seat of the Farquharsons dates from the fifteenth century although a new wing and tower were added in 1874.

Ballater, centre touristique le plus important de l'Upper Deeside (58), jouit d'une situation abritée non loin du confluent de la rivière Muick avec la Dee. Un des bâtiments les plus impressionnants des Highlands est le château Craigievar (59), qui fut construit au dix-septième siècle. Avec ses tours rondes et ses innombrables tourelles il rappelle les châteaux français. Le château de Balmoral (60) fut acheté par le Prince Consort pour la reine Victoria, qui fit reconstruire le château et en agrandit le domaine. C'est une résidence royale depuis 1855.

Ballater, das wichtigste Touristenzentrum des oberen Deetals (58), hat eine geschützte Lage am Zusammenfluß der Muick und der Dee. Eines der eindrucksvollsten Gebäude des Hochlands ist Schloß Craigievar (59), das im 17. Jahrhundert erbaut wurde. Mit seinen vielen runden Türmen und vielen Türmchen gleicht es einem französischen Schloß. Schloß Balmoral (60) wurde für die Königin Victoria von dem Prinzgemahl Albert gekauft; er ließ das Schloß umbauen und das Gut vergrößern. Seit 1855 ist es eine königliche Residenz.

58

59

The important tourist resort of Ballater (58) is situated seventeen miles further down the valley from Braemar, near the confluence of the Dee and the River Muick. This is the chief centre of Upper Deeside. The Dee by now has grown broader and is encircled by pleasantly wooded hills, although the district is dominated by the snow-capped peak of Lochnagar, 3,786 feet high. Glen Muick (the 'Glen of the Pig') stretches south-west of Ballater to the Lochnagar range. This glen was much loved by Queen Victoria, and the royal residence of Birkhall, purchased by Edward VII, stands here.

One of the most impressive buildings in the Highlands is Craigievar Castle (59), six miles south of Alford. The style of this early seventeenth-century castle, seven storeys high, is reminiscent of a French château, with its rounded towers and turrets. The interior contains a fine hall with a beautiful Renaissance ceiling and an inscription above the fireplace 'Doe not vaiken sleeping dogs'.

Deeside became 'Royal' in the second half of the nineteenth century when Balmoral Castle (60), situated on the south bank of the River Dee, was bought by the Prince Consort for Queen Victoria. She had the castle rebuilt in white granite and also extended the estate by incorporating the Ballochbuie Forest into it. Balmoral Castle was first occupied by the Royal Family in 1855 and the court has been in residence here for a part of each year ever since. The castle itself is not open to the public but its extensive grounds, where rolling lawns complement the wooded hills, can be visited at certain times during the summer.

61

La rivière Dee (61) commence son cours assez haut dans les Cairngorms pareil à un cours d'eau sauvage des Highlands, puis elle descend plus doucement jusqu'à Balmoral où alors elle jouit du titre de Royal Deeside, et enfin elle continue son cours jusqu'à Ballater, si populaire (62). Enfin, la Dee, excellente rivière pour le saumon, se retire entièrement des Highlands. La route de Lecht (63), que l'on peut atteindre par le Deeside, traverse un paysage sauvage pour atteindre Tomintoul, un des villages les plus hauts de l'Ecosse.

Der Fluß Dee (61) entspringt als wilder Hochlandbach in den Cairngorms und fließt dann ruhiger nach Balmoral, wo er den Titel „Royal Deeside" trägt, und weiter zum beliebten Touristenort Ballater (62). Schließlich verläßt die Dee, die für den Lachsfang berühmt ist, das Hochland. Die „Lecht Road" (63), die durch Deeside zu erreichen ist, führt durch eine wilde Landschaft nach Tomintoul, einem der höchst gelegenen Dörfer Schottlands.

The River Dee (61) begins its tremendous journey high up in the range of the Cairngorm mountains (its main source is at the Wells of Dee on Einich Cairn) as a wild Highland stream, and its waters fall more than 2,000 feet before finally entering the sea at Aberdeen. The Linn of Dee, near Inverey, is especially fascinating, for here the river rushes under a tiny bridge to cascade over huge slabs of rock and swirl into a narrow cleft where salmon can be seen frantically leaping from gorge to gorge. By the time the river has reached Balmoral, it has broadened out into a beautiful wooded valley which well deserves its title of 'Royal Deeside'. This most famous stretch of the Dee extends approximately from Braemar to the popular resort of Ballater (62). Below the richly wooded banks of Ballater, the Dee begins to lose its wild Highland character as it winds its way towards the open sea. Excellent motoring roads run for much of the way along the Dee, offering extensive views of the coarse, heathery grouse moors, and the occasional glimpse of a majestic red deer.

The Lecht Road (63), which can be easily reached from Deeside, starts from Cock Bridge on the Dee's twin river, the Don. This is part of a military road dating from 1754, and crosses the north-easterly portion of the Grampians. Motorists should drive carefully here, for the road has a maximum gradient of 1 in 5 and reaches a height of 2,090 feet, gradually descending until it comes to Tomintoul, the Highlands' highest village at 1,160 feet.

Highland Region

The Highland Region, the largest and most remote county of Great Britain, includes the former districts of Caithness, Sutherland, Ross and Cromarty, Nairn and Inverness.

The northernmost portion of this region is one of Britain's last wildernesses and, fortunately, it is the least likely ever to be despoiled. Many thousands of square miles of wonderful countryside lie remote from any road. Everywhere one looks, the pinnacles of precipitous mountains rear over dark and mystical lochs, whose waters reflect the myriad hues of the mountain flanks, clad in purple heather. The stormy western Atlantic coast is indented with innumerable sea-lochs of all shapes and sizes while, at strategic points on their shores, small townships are situated where men may follow the twin callings of fishing and agriculture. The northern coast of Scotland is even wilder and less accessible, and includes the great sea-lochs of Kyle of Durness, Loch Eriboll and the Kyle of Tongue. The North Sea coast is less savage and, although still immensely beautiful, the mountains here lack the lonely grandeur of those to the west.

Further south, around Inverness, the region is less stern and forbidding though it is still, in the words of Sir Walter Scott, 'a land of brown heath and shaggy wood, land of the mountain and the flood'. Here, in the magnificent Great Glen, Lochs Lochy, Oich and Ness are linked by twenty-one miles of artificial waterway, the Caledonian Canal, which Thomas Telford built early last century.

The Highland Region now also includes the beautiful Isle of Skye off Scotland's western coast; truly a magical place whose name, in Gaelic, means 'the Isle of Mist'. Here, Bonnie Prince Charlie fled after his defeat at Culloden in 1746. Its coastline is some 300 miles long, deeply indented by sea-lochs, while the most remarkable of the many mountains to be found here are the jagged peaks of the Cuillins range, over 3,000 feet high.

The River Shiel and the twin peaks of the 'Saddle'.
La rivière Shiel at les pics jumeaux de la « Selle ».
Der Fluß Shiel und die Zwillingsgipfel des „Sattels".

The appearance of the great mass of granite, lava and schists that make up Ben Nevis can be rather deceptive for it seems broad rather than high yet, at 4,406 feet, Ben Nevis is the highest mountain in the British Isles. It has no actual peak but its principal summit is topped by a cairn made from stones brought from Everest, Kilimanjaro and many other places. An observatory and an hotel once stood here also. Despite its height, the ascent is quite easy, though one should be prepared for a five-mile climb. The northern flanks of Ben Nevis are scarred with incredible corries – here (64) its slopes, streaked with snow throughout much of the year, are seen from Corpach at the head of Loch Linnhe.

The wild scenery of Glen Coe was the setting for the massacre of the Macdonalds by the Campbells in 1692. Glen Coe today, though it still bears the scars of the tragedy, is a beautiful valley stretching from Rannoch Moor to Loch Leven. The Pap of Glencoe (or Sgor na Criche), 2,430 feet, a strange mountain with a barren peak, guards the entrance to the glen (65). The 'Three Sisters' of Glencoe – Aonach Dubh, Gearr Aonach and Ben Fhada – raise their gaunt pinnacles above Loch Achtriochtan. The legendary Gaelic bard Ossian was apparently born on the shores of this loch – here (66) we see it overshadowed by the massive sweep of Chancellor Ridge.

The sea-loch of Loch Leven (67) borders Glen Coe to the north and extends almost twenty miles from Loch Linnhe to Kinlochleven. It can be crossed by ferry from Ballachulish. Loch Leven is fed by tributaries that drop sheer from the mighty ridges on either hand: one of these tributaries is the River Coe, which lends its name to the glen.

La montagne Ben Nevis avec son bonnet blanc est avec ses 1 348 mètres la plus haute des îles britanniques. Cette vue du flanc sud (64) a été prise du village de Corpach qui se trouve près du goulet qui sépare Loch Eil de Loch Linnhe. Le mamelon de Glencoe, 741 mètres, qui surveille plus en bas Loch Leven (65), garde l'entrée nord-ouest de la passe qui traverse les montagnes. Loch Achtriochtan (66) est ombragé par le Chancellor Ridge, tandis que plus haut, sur Aonach Dubh, on trouve la fente connue sous le nom de la caverne d'Ossian d'après le poète légendaire gaélique. Sur deux des îles du magnifique Loch Leven (67) on aperçoit les ruines d'un prieuré et d'un château du quinzième siècle.

Der schneegekrönte Ben Nevis, 1 348 m, ist der höchste Berg Großbritanniens. Hier (64) blickt man auf seinen Südhang vom Dorf Corpach aus, das auf einer engen Landspitze zwischen Loch Eil und Loch Linnhe liegt. Der „Pap of Glencoe", 741 m, der auf Loch Leven blickt (65), schützt den nordwestlichen Passeingang. Loch Achtriochtan (66) wird von dem „Chancellor Ridge" überschattet; oberhalb, auf Aonach Dubh, befindet sich eine Spalte, genannt „Ossian's Cave", nach einem legendären gälischen Barden. In dem schönen Loch Leven (67) stehen auf zwei Inseln die Ruinen eines Klosters und eines Schlosses aus dem 15. Jahrhundert.

65   66

69 70

Les ruines du château de Tioram (68) du treizième
siècle surveille Loch Moidart: l'île est reliée au rivage à
marée basse. Aviemore (69), sur la vallée de la Spey, est
un centre sportif populaire avec des pentes de ski magnifiques à proximité (70). Loch Shiel aux eaux si pures
est entouré de montagnes altières (71). Fort William (72)
sur le Loch Linnhe fut à une certaine époque l'emplacement d'un fort construit par le Général Monk en 1655.
Ce monument imposant (73) fut érigé à Spean Bridge
en mémoire des troupes qui furent formées ici.

Aus dem 13. Jahrhundert stammen die Ruinen des
Schlosses Tioram (68), die Loch Moidart überwachen;
bei Ebbe ist die Insel von dem Ufer zu erreichen.
Aviemore (69) im Speytal ist ein beliebtes Sportzentrum
mit herrlichem Skigelände (70). Der Süßwasser-Loch
Shiel ist von hohen Bergen umgeben (71). In Fort
William (72), am Loch Linnhe, stand einst eine Festung,
die 1655 von dem General Monk erbaut wurde. Dieses
imposante Denkmal (73) wurde bei Spean Bridge
errichtet, zur Erinnerung an die Kommandotruppen,
die hier trainierten.

71

Loch Moidart is a narrow sea-inlet lying by the western end of Loch Shiel. At its mouth rests the great island of Eilean Shona, while its waters are guarded by the ruins of the thirteenth-century Castle Tioram (68) which once belonged to the MacDonalds of Clanranald. The castle is joined to the shore by a sand-spit, although this is submerged at high tide.

The greatest winter sports centre in the Highlands is Aviemore (69), a village in Strathspey. It owes its popularity to the fact that it is the nearest village to the Cairngorms and thus is an excellent base for those who wish to ski on these mountains (70). Aviemore's attractions are not confined to the winter, however, for it now has its own pleasure complex offering numerous facilities, while the more energetic can visit the nearby forests of Rothiemurchus and Abernethy.

Loch Shiel, bordered by stern mountains (71), is a freshwater loch stretching the eighteen miles from Glenfinnan to Acharacle. Despite its length, it is a narrow loch, never exceeding one mile in width. The area holds many associations with Bonnie Prince Charlie, for on 19 August 1745, the Prince unfurled his standard at Glenfinnan to mark the beginning of the Rising. The Prince Charles Edward Monument, shown on the right of this photograph, was erected in 1815 by the descendant of one of his supporters in memory of the Highlanders who followed the Prince. The Monument takes the form of a simple round tower surmounted by the figure of a Highlander.

Fort William (72), dominated by the summit of Ben Nevis, lies at the south end of the Great Glen. The original fort was founded in 1654 by General Monk but was later rebuilt and named Fort William after William III. However, it was demolished in 1864 and only the gateway now remains. A road leads from Fort William to Spean Bridge, about ten miles away. General Wade built a bridge here but the existing one was erected by Telford in 1812. This dramatic Commando Memorial stands by the bridge (73), facing Ben Nevis, in honour of the Commandos of the Second World War, who trained here.

72   73

Fort Augustus (74) se trouve en tête de Loch Ness. Le fort original fut établi ici par le Général Wade en 1730 pour commander les routes qu'il fit construire à travers Great Glen et par-dessus la passe de Corrieyairack. De nos jours c'est un endroit propice à la pêche. Les routes parallèles du Glen Roy (75) forment une série étrange de récifs sur les collines sculptées par l'érosion glaciaire. En dépit de l'introduction d'un plan hydro-électrique, Glen Affric (76), avec ses rïvières au courant torrentueux, est toujours un glen splendide qui est resté presqu'entièrement non-endommagé. L'île de Skye est la plus grande et la plus connue de toutes les îles d'Ecosse. De Bracadale, le visiteur à Skye peut admirer les magnifiques Black Cuillins de l'autre côté de Loch Harport (77).

75

Fort Augustus (74) liegt am oberen Ende des Loch Ness. Die ursprüngliche Festung wurde hier 1730 von General Wade errichtet, um die Landstraßen, die er durch das „Great Glen" und über den Paß von Corrieyairack baute, zu beherrschen. Heute ist sie ein Ferienort für Angler. Die „Parallel Roads" des Glen Roy (75) sind sonderbare Felssimse, die durch Gletschereinwirkung entstanden sind. Trotz des Baues eines Wasserkraftsystems in Glen Affric (76) bleibt dieses schöne Tal mit seinem tobenden Fluß fast ganz unverdorben. Die Insel Skye ist die größte und bekannteste aller schottischen Inseln. Von Bracadale aus kann der Besucher die prächtigen „Black Cuillins" über Loch Harport (77) erblicken.

76

Fort Augustus is a superbly situated village at the head of Loch Ness, near the point where the famous Caledonian Canal enters the loch. The village has an exciting history, for, after the 1715 Jacobite rising, the English erected some barracks here which were converted into an actual fort in 1730 by General Wade. The site had previously been called Kilcummin but it was now rechristened Fort Augustus after William Augustus, Duke of Cumberland. The fort was connected to Speyside by Wade's great road, the Corrieyairack Pass, now only accessible to the most energetic of walkers. In 1746 Fort Augustus was taken by the Highlanders but was quickly recovered by the English government after the Battle of Culloden. During the nineteenth century, a Benedictine abbey was founded here and is still in use, while Fort Augustus today (74) is a popular angling resort. Loch Ness, though undeniably very beautiful, is best known for the elusive monster supposed to haunt its murky depths. The loch is twenty-four miles long and, because it is so deep (700 feet in places), it has never been known to freeze.

One of the most amazing sights in Scotland are the Parallel Roads of Glen Roy. Situated by Roy Bridge, these 'Roads' are, in fact, a parallel series of ledges along the hill-sides, clearly seen from this viewpoint (75). The upper ledges are about eighty feet apart – the highest, of course, are the oldest. These natural phenomena are a product of glacial action, for they are the beaches of former lakes.

Glen Affric (76) stretches from the mountains of Kintail to the valley of Strath Glass, west of Loch Ness, and its river flows through Loch Affric and Loch Beneveian. Despite the introduction of a hydro-electric power scheme here in 1952, this beautiful glen has remained almost unspoilt.

Skye, largest of the Hebrides, is one of the most romantic islands in Britain. Despite its size, no point is further than five miles from the sea. From Bracadale, the visitor can gaze across Loch Harport to the jagged pinnacles of the Cuillins (77).

77

A range of distant mountains, shimmering in a misty haze, set off the tranquil beauty of Loch Glascarnoch (78), yet this is really an artificial loch, with a dam at its lower end. One of the most amazing mountains in the Highlands is Liathach, 3,456 feet high, seen here towering over Upper Loch Torridon (79). Its name, which means 'the grey one', is rather misleading for Liathach is really a sheer mass of red 'Torridonian' sandstone, naturally terraced along its side, with a contrasting cap of snowy white quartzite. Its ridge is over three miles long.

Eilean Donan Castle (80) stands proudly on a small island in Loch Long, though it is now joined to the shore by a causeway. The castle, which was founded in 1230, was first attacked in 1539; and later, in 1719, bombarded by English ships – it was reduced to ruins but was extensively restored in 1932.

Le splendide Loch Glascarnoch (78) est en fait un loch artificiel avec un barrage sur sa partie la plus basse. Liathach, 1 053 mètres, est une montagne de grès massive rougeâtre (79) avec un sommet qui contraste par son quartz blanc. Upper Loch Torridon se trouve à son pied et offre une vue magnifique de la montagne. Le château d'Eilean Donan (80) fut construit en 1230 et fut utilisé comme forteresse par le Clan des MacRae. Il fut attaqué à deux reprises et laissé en ruines jusqu'à ce qu'il fut restauré en 1932 et par la suite ouvert aux visiteurs. Autrefois le château était entouré d'eau, mais il est de nos jours relié au rivage du Loch Long.

Der wunderschöne Glascarnoch Loch, von auffallender Berglandschaft umgeben (78), ist jedoch ein künstlicher See mit einer Talsperre am unteren Ende. In der Nähe liegt der Kinlochluichart Forest. Liathach, 1 053 m, ist ein massiver Berg aus rotem Sandstein (79), mit einem kontrastierenden Gipfel aus weißem Quarzit, der über Glen Torridon emporragt. Am Fuße liegt Upper Loch Torridon, von wo man einen umfassenden Blick auf den Berg genießt. Das 1230 gegründete Schloß Eilean Donan (80) wurde als Festung von dem Klan MacRae benutzt. Es wurde zweimal angegriffen und zerstört, bis es 1932 restauriert und zur Besichtigung freigegeben wurde. Das Schloß war einst von Wasser umgeben, aber heute ist es mit dem Ufer des Loch Long verbunden.

78

81

82

Loch Broom, un bras de mer profond (81),
s'enfonce assez loin dans les collines. Sur son
rivage se trouve le village de pêcheurs d'Ullapool.
De l'indicateur de Struie Hill on a une vue magnifique sur le Dornoch Firth (82). Deux rivières
coulent dans la baie de Gruinard qui est sur-
plombée par une colline aux pentes raides (83).
Loch Kanaird (84) est un petit bras de mer.
Plocton, un village avec de petits cottages sur le
Loch Carron (85), s'est octroyé une certaine
renommée pour la navigation de plaisance.

Loch Broom, eine tiefe Meeresbucht (81), reicht
weit in die Hügel. An dem Ufer liegt das Fischer-
dorf Ullapool. Bei dem Wegweiser auf Struie Hill,
über dem Dornoch Firth (82), genießt man einen
herrlichen Blick. Zwei Flüsse fließen in die
Gruinard Bay, die von einem steilen Hügel
überragt ist (83). Łoch Kanaird (84) ist eine
kleine Meeresbucht. Plockton, ein Kleinbauern-
dorf am Loch Carron (85), ist ein sehr beliebtes
Zentrum für Jachtsportler.

83

84

Loch Broom (81) is a deep inlet of the sea with the fine scenery of the Strath More Valley at its head. On its north shore stands Ullapool, a pleasant resort which was founded in 1788 as a centre for the herring fishing industry. Herring fishing, along with lobsters and white fish, still flourishes today here, as does the tourist trade.

Broad Dornoch Firth, into which projects a narrow spit of land known as Dornoch Point, is bounded on each side by green and fertile plains. The sweeping view from the indicator at Struie Hill (82) looking across the Dornoch Firth is particularly fine, and yet the height here is only about 700 feet above sea-level.

One of the chief beauty spots in the north-west Highlands is Gruinard Bay, situated on the main routeway from Poolewe to Ullapool. Here (83), grey rocky outcrops are set amidst low but rugged hills, while two rivers, the Gruinard and the Little Gruinard, descend on the bay. Offshore is Gruinard Island, which was unfortunately contaminated with anthrax during wartime experiments and so is closed to visitors. Off the north side of Loch Broom is another little bay, known as Loch Kanaird (84). This illustration shows Ardmair Bay on Loch Kanaird looking south to Beinn Ghobhlach over the Rhu peninsula.

Plockton (85) is a large crofting, fishing and yachting centre which sits in a sheltered cove by Loch Carron. This loch lies in the lower part of Glen Carron, which stretches through the beautiful Achnashellach Forest. Nearby is the nineteenth-century Duncraig Castle, now a school.

The village of Lochinver, which straggles along the shore of the sea-loch of the same name, affords a remarkable view of the 2,399-foot high Suilven (86) sometimes known as the 'Matterhorn' of Scotland. The panorama from the summit of its massive, double-peaked 'sugar-loaf' dome shows a multitude of tiny lochans unfolding over the countryside, with the Glencanisp Forest to the south and the isles of Harris and Lewis far out to sea.

Loch Glencoul (87) is seen to its best advantage by boat, since there is no good road around its barren shores. Glencoul and its sister Loch Glendhu converge upon the great sea-inlet of Loch Cairnbawn, which can be crossed on the ferry operating from Kylesku. The scenery surrounding all three lochs is reminiscent of the Norwegian fjords. Badcall (88) is a small and almost self-sufficient hamlet of crofts scattered around an enchanting, island-studded bay. The surrounding mountains, including Quinag, Glasven, Ben Stack and Arkle, are interspersed with desolate moorlands where the shaggy Highland cattle roam freely. The last wolf in Scotland is said to have been killed here.

Le village de Lochinver se trouve à l'écart sur le rivage du loch de mer du même nom. Les vues des alentours de Loch Inver sont splendides, mais toutefois le spectacle le plus impressionnant reste celui de l'énorme et insolite dome de Suilven, 731 mètres (86). Loch Glencoul (87), comparable en apparence à un fjord norvégien, peut être le mieux vu par bateau car il n'y a pas de route ici. Tout près se trouve Kylesku, où l'on peut traverser les eaux de Loch Cairnbawn par ferry. Le village de Badcall (88) se compose de quelques petits cottages avec une vue splendide sur la baie.

Das Dorf Lochinver schlängelt sich am Ufer des Meeresarms gleichen Namens entlang. Die Aussichten um Loch Inver sind herrlich, doch der eindruckvollste Anblick ist die riesige und ungewöhnlich geformte Kuppel des Suilven, 731 m (86). Loch Glencoul (87), das einem norwegischen Fjord gleicht, kann man am besten von einem Boot aus sehen, da es hier keine Straße gibt. In der Nähe liegt Kylesku, von wo man Loch Cairnbawn, der sich Loch Glencoul anschließt, kostenlos mit einer Auto- und Personenfähre überqueren kann. Das Dorf Badcall (88) besteht aus einigen zerstreut gelegenen kleinen Bauernhöfen. Von hier hat man einen wunderbaren Blick über die Bucht.

88

Loch a'Chairn Bhain, also known as Loch Cairnbawn (89) is a sea-inlet at Eddrachillis Bay. Its upper reaches are strewn with islands, above which the loch divides into the two arms of Lochs Glencoul and Glendhu. The narrows where they meet are crossed by car ferry from Kylesku. The loch was used as a submarine base during the Second World War but today its calm waters have nothing to conceal. Well worth a visit is the nearby Eascoul-Aulin, a 658-foot-high waterfall which is about three times as high as Niagara. Loch Eriboll (90) is also an arm of the sea, some ten miles long, which provides a safe anchorage for vessels on this storm-tossed coast. The great peaks of Grann Stacach, 2,630 feet, and Beinn Spionnaidh, 2,537 feet, cluster around the head of this beautiful loch, while the smaller Craig-na-Faoilinn, 934 feet, has a majestic rolling echo.

Here (91), the sun sets over Tongue Bay at the entrance to the shallow Kyle of Tongue. 'Kyle' is a Gaelic word meaning 'strait'. Just offshore are Rabbit Island and Eilean nan Ron, the latter of which was inhabited by fifty people about a hundred years ago. The last islanders (four men and three women) left in 1938. Nearby stand the ruins of Castle Varrich, said to have been the stronghold of an eleventh-century Norse king. The little village of Forsinard (92) lies in the heart of the lonely moorland country crossed by Straths Halladale and Ullie – Strath Halladale was the former boundary between the Sutherland and Mackay clans. Despite its isolation, Forsinard is well known for its excellent fishing and its lamb sales.

Le bras de mer de Loch a'Chairn Bhain, connu parfois sous le nom de Loch Cairnbawn (89), se divise en deux bras jumeaux, Loch Glendhu et Loch Glencoul. Tous trois sont entourés par un paysage de montagnes formidable. Loch Eriboll (90) est aussi un bras de mer, de quelque seize kilomètres de long, qui offre aux navires un point d'ancrage sûr sur cette côte battue par les tempêtes. Ici (91) l'on voit le soleil se coucher sur la baie de Tongue à l'entrée de Kyle of Tongue. Tout proche du rivage sont les îles Rabbit et Eilean nan Ron. Forsinard (92) est un petit village isolé au cœur de ces landes désertes. Il est surveillé par les montagnes Ben Griam Beg et Ben Grim Mhor.

Die kleine Meeresbucht Loch a' Chairn Bhain (89), auch Loch Cairnbawn genannt, teilt sich in zwei Arme, den Loch Glendhu und Loch Glencoul. Alle drei sind von einer eindrucksvollen Berglandschaft umgeben. Loch Eriboll (90) ist ebenfalls eine Meeresbucht. Mit einer Länge von 16 km bietet er, an dieser stürmischen Küste, einen sicheren Ankerplatz für Schiffe. Hier (91) sieht man einen Sonnenuntergang über Tongue Bay, nahe dem Zugang zum Kyle of Tongue. Nahe der Küste liegen zwei Inseln, „ Rabbit Island" und Eilean Nan Ron. Forsinard (92) ist ein Dorf mitten in einer einsamen Hochmoorlandschaft. Es wird von den Bergen Ben Griam Beg Grim Mhor überblickt.

90

92

The wild and desolate Loch Hope is watched over by the snowy heights of Ben Hope, 3,040 feet, Scotland's most northerly peak of over 3,000 feet. This picture (93) was taken from the track that climbs over the shoulder between Lochs Eriboll and Hope: it is quite impassable by car but the scenery is exhilarating. Although not so high, the Quinag (94) is equally impressive as a landmark. This mountain has seven peaks, the highest of which is 2,653 feet, and they are linked by a ridge which makes an exciting walk. Its name (spelt Cuinneag in Gaelic) means 'churn' or 'pail'. Here it is seen from the road below Loch Ganvich.

Stoer is a remote village surrounded by tiny lochans and a sweeping bay. The view from a point above the bay (95) commands the distant peaks of Cul Mor, Cul Beag and Stack Polly. The road to Lairg from Tongue (one that is frequently snowed up in winter) runs beside the beautiful waters of Loch Loyal (96). The most prominent feature of the landscape for many miles around the Kyle of Tongue is the splendid range of granite peaks known collectively as Ben Loyal.

John o' Groats is often taken to be Britain's most northerly point, but in reality Dunnet Head (97) is further north and has a more impressive character. A lonely lighthouse clings to the edge of this rugged promontory and it performs a vitally necessary function, for here the stormy waters of the Atlantic meet those of the North Sea. Dunnet Head is separated from the Old Man of Hoy and the Orkneys by the storm-wracked Pentland Firth.

93

94

96

Le solitaire et désolé Loch Hope est gardé par les sommets de Ben Hope, 927 mètres (93). Le Quinag, 809 mètres (94), présente sept pics bien distincts qui sont tous reliés par des écueils. La vue que l'on aperçoit au-delà de la baie de Stoer (95) est formée des sommets de Cul Mor, Cul Beag et Stack Polly. Loch Loyal (96) est entouré d'une série de pics de granit qui sont connus sous le nom de Ben Loyal. Le promontoire sauvage de Dunnet Head (97) est le point de terre ferme situé le plus au nord de la Grande-Bretagne.

Der einsame, verlassene Loch Hope wird von dem schneebedeckten Ben Hope, 927 m (93), bewacht. „The Quinag", 809 m (94), hat sieben deutliche Gipfel, die durch einen Grat verbunden sind. Oberhalb der „Bay of Stoer" (95) kann man auch die entfernten Gipfel von Cul Mor, Cul Beag und Stack Polly sehen. Loch Loyal (96) ist von einer Kette imposanter Granitgipfel umgeben, die Ben Loyal heißt. Das wilde, schroffe Vorgebirge „Dunnet Head" (97) ist der nördlichst gelegene Zipfel des Großbritannischen Festlandes.

97

At picturesque Berriedale (98), two wooded glens and their waters meet by the ruins of a castle which was once the stronghold of the Earls of Caithness. The little village of Berriedale can boast of some unusual buildings which are imaginatively decorated with numerous antlers. In the distance loom the magical snow-capped peaks of Scaraben, 2,054 feet, and Morven, 2,313 feet high, silhouetted against the cold blue sky.

John o' Groats (99) is Scotland's answer to Land's End. Although this is not, in fact, Britain's most northerly point, it still proves a great attraction to visitors. The unusual name is derived from John de Groot, a Dutchman who, in the fifteenth century, operated a ferry to Orkney from this spot. Later, eight descendants laid claim to his estate and, to avoid friction, an octagonal house with eight entrances was built, containing an octagonal table so that each could sit at its head. Unfortunately, the house is no longer standing, though a flagpole marks its former site. The beach here is of white sand, scattered with small shells known as Groatie Buckies, and just offshore lies the island of Stroma, with the Orkneys beyond.

Au pittoresque Berriedale (98), près des ruines d'un château, deux glens boisés se rencontrent alors que dans le lointain se dessinent les pics de Scaraben et de Morven. Le nom insolite de John o' Groats provient de John de Groot, un hollandais qui opéra un ferry à cet emplacement (99) au quinzième siècle.

Im malerischen Berriedale (98) treffen sich zwei bewaldete Täler neben den Ruinen eines Schlosses; in der Ferne ragen die Gipfel von Scaraben und Morven empor. Der Name ,,John o' Groats" erinnert an einen Holländer, der im 15. Jahrhundert hier eine Fähre bediente (99).

SBN 85306 600 0
© 1975 Jarrold & Sons Ltd, Norwich
Printed and bound in Great Britain by
Jarrold & Sons Ltd, Norwich. 175